First Look:
Science

Take a Walk on a Rainbow

A First Look at Color

by Miriam Moss   illustrated by Amanda Wood

Thanks to our reading adviser:

Susan Kesselring, M.A., Literacy Educator
Rosemount-Apple Valley-Eagan (Minnesota) School District

PICTURE WINDOW BOOKS
Minneapolis, Minnesota

First American edition published in 2005 by
Picture Window Books
5115 Excelsior Boulevard
Suite 232
Minneapolis, MN 55416
877-845-8392
www.picturewindowbooks.com

First published in Great Britain in 1999 by McDonald Young Books,
an imprint of Wayland Publishers Ltd.
61 Western Road
Hove
East Sussex
BN3 1JD

Printed in the United States of America.

Library of Congress Cataloging-in-Publication Data
Moss, Miriam.
Take a walk on a rainbow : a first look at color / by Miriam Moss;
illustrated by Amanda Wood.
p. cm. — (First look : science)
ISBN 1-4048-0660-1
1. Colors—Juvenile literature. I. Wood, Amanda, ill. II. Title.
III. Series.
QC495.5.M67 2005
535.6—dc22   2004007314

For Fergus – M.M.
For Rosie and her friends in Miss Bailey's class – A.W.

Storm clouds gather, and the sky turns black.

4

When there's no light, there's no color.

5

CRACK! Lightning flashes,

6

and Tracy's room lights up with color.

made up of all the colors of the rainbow.

making the sunlight spread out into all the colors of the rainbow.

Birds can see many colors. Cats, dogs, and

horses only see in black, white, and gray.

17

Look at that red frog, Grandpa!

The bright red color of the

poisonous frog warns the monkey not to touch it.

24

25

fades, and everything looks black and gray again.

27

Mix It Up!

The light that shines from the sun looks white, but it's really made up of all the colors of the rainbow.

See for yourself when you spin this simple color wheel. All the colors will mix together and look white before your eyes!

To make the wheel:

1. Cut out a circle of heavy paper.

2. Color it like this:

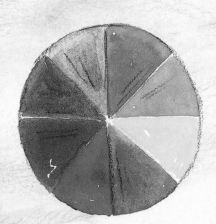

3. Stick a pencil through the middle.

4. Spin it!

Useful Words

Chameleon
A small lizard living in hot countries. A chameleon can hide by changing its skin to the same color as the things around it.

Lightning
Giant flashes of light that break out of thunderclouds during a storm. You can see the lightning flash before you hear the sound of thunder.

Rainbow
An arch in the sky made of lots of colors. A rainbow appears when white light from the sun shines through raindrops in the air. The raindrops make white light spread out into all the colors of the rainbow.

Storm
Bad weather. There can be strong winds, rain or snow, and sometimes thunder and lightning.

Fun Facts

 An easy way to remember the colors of the rainbow is to spell Roy G. Biv—red, orange, yellow, green, blue, indigo, violet.

 The three primary colors are red, yellow, and blue. They are the only colors that can't be made by mixing two other colors.

 The three secondary colors are green, orange, and violet. These colors are made by mixing two primary colors.

 Black, white, and gray are not true colors. They are called neutral colors.

To Learn More

At the Library

Hoban, Tana. *Colors Everywhere.* New York: Greenwillow Books, 1995.

Letzig, Michael. *The Crayon Box that Talked.* New York: Random House, 1997.

Siomades, Lorianne. *My Box of Color.* Honesdale, Pa.: Boyds Mill Press, 1998.

On the Web

FactHound offers a safe, fun way to find Web sites related to this book. All of the sites on FactHound have been researched by our staff. *www.facthound.com*

1. Visit the FactHound home page.
2. Enter a search word related to this book, or type in this special code: 1404806601.
3. Click the FETCH IT button.

Your trusty FactHound will fetch the best Web sites for you!

Index

color wheel, 28, 29

light, 5, 7, 12, 26, 28

lightning, 6, 30

rainbow, 9, 10, 11, 26, 28, 30, 31

raindrops, 10

sky, 4

storm, 4, 30

sunlight, 8, 11

Look for all the books in this series:

A Seed in Need
A First Look at the Plant Cycle

And Everyone Shouted, "Pull!"
A First Look at Forces of Motion

From Little Acorns ...
A First Look at the Life Cycle of a Tree

Paint a Sun in the Sky
A First Look at the Seasons

Take a Walk on a Rainbow
A First Look at Color

The Case of the Missing Caterpillar
A First Look at the Life Cycle of a Butterfly

The Drop Goes Plop
A First Look at the Water Cycle

The Hen Can't Help It
A First Look at the Life Cycle of a Chicken

The Trouble with Tadpoles
A First Look at the Life Cycle of a Frog